YoungWriters PRESENTS

MONSTER ACROSTICS

Poetic Creatures

First published in Great Britain in 2025 by:

YoungWriters®
Est. 1991

Young Writers
Remus House
Coltsfoot Drive
Peterborough
PE2 9BF
Telephone: 01733 890066
Website: www.youngwriters.co.uk

All Rights Reserved
Book Design by Neila Cepulionyte
© Copyright Contributors 2025
Softback ISBN 978-1-83685-509-5
Printed and bound in the UK by BookPrintingUK
Website: www.bookprintinguk.com
YB0642W

Foreword

Welcome Reader,

For Young Writers' latest competition Monster Acrostics, we asked primary school pupils to create a monster then write an acrostic poem about it. The acrostic is a fantastic introduction to poetry writing as it comes with a built-in structure, allowing children to focus on their creativity and vocabulary choice.

We live and breathe creativity here at Young Writers and we want to pass our love of the written word onto the next generation – what better way to do that than to celebrate their writing by publishing it in a book!

Featuring all kinds of crazy creatures, strange beasts and mythical monsters, this anthology is brimming with imagination and creativity, showcasing the blossoming writing skills of these young poets. They have brought their creations to life using the power of words, resulting in some brilliant and fun acrostic poems!

Each awesome little poet in this book should be super proud of themselves! We hope you will delight in these poems as much as we have.

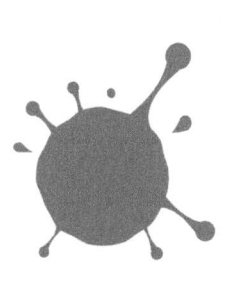

Contents

Alpha Preparatory School, Harrow

Ahaan Bhavnani (6)	1
Vishaan Kansagra (5)	2
Rohan Haria-Collins (6)	3
Yanle Li (5)	4
Neil Bhudia (5)	5
Yichen Shi (7)	6
Jinyao Xu (6)	7
Adam Rashid (6)	8
Sai Patel (6)	9
Priyen Lakhani (7)	10
Sienna Patil (6)	11
Yashvi Pindoria (7)	12
Veer Kathrecha (6)	13
Daaris Siddiqui (7)	14
Rezaan Lasharie (7)	15
Khaydan Patel (6)	16
Zak Patel (6)	17
Dylan Kharaud-Patel (6)	18
Ryan Mara (6)	19
Amilia Rajendram (5)	20
Ammar Banire (5)	21
Purvi Udupi (5)	22
Kaiyan Patel (6)	23
Ishaan Verma (6)	24
Jesse Pinduria (5)	25
Satvik Kashyap (5)	26

Callander Primary School, Bridgend

Eddy-Joe Kidd (7)	27
Noah Beaton (6)	28
Louis Nicholson (7)	29

Daniel Wood (6)	30
Faith Glen (6)	31
Ruby Macmillan-Rae (6)	32
Morven McSorley (6)	33
Solomon Walker-Cunliffe (6)	34
Fergus Picken (6)	35
Joseph Cox (7)	36
Laura Wasyluk (7)	37
Tilly Burke (7)	38

Hazlehead Primary School, Aberdeen

Arran Small (7)	39
Matthew Speagell (7)	40
Emma Axinti (7)	41
Yaseen Hegy (7)	42
Abbie Rostant (7)	43
Brayden Mackie (7)	44
Anna Garrett (7)	45
Asya Konaroglu (7)	46
Whitney Kaka (7)	47
Jessica Smith (7)	48
Demians Blazevics (7)	49
Skye-Marie Anderson (8)	50
Jessica Cheyne (7)	51
Finn Teperek (7)	52
Aleksandra Firsovas (7)	53
Rowan McKay (7)	54
Jasper Houston (7)	55
Spencer Chapman (8)	56
Eve McCarry (7)	57
Finn Hewitt (7)	58
Poppy McCombie (7)	59
Hope Thomson (8)	60
Maci Wood (8)	61

Lexi Smith (7)	62
Thomas Gray (7)	63
Lewis Hume (7)	64
William McAulay (7)	65
Manish Shatheesh (7)	66
Erin Macdonald (7)	67
Nicholas Taylor (7)	68

ILM Primary School, Cathays

Rayaan Ismail (5)	69
Zara Noor (5)	70
Haroon Idris (5)	71
Yusuf Tahir (4)	72
Faraj Islam (5)	73
Maryam Saeed (5)	74
Maryam Tarafder (4)	75
Shuaib Mohamed (4)	76
Reem Alhayfani (5)	77
Azees Jan De Jager Khan (4)	78
Muhammad Abdur Raheem (5)	79
Haneen Haseeb (4)	80
Bilal Aziz (4)	81
Raheem Nassar Ismail (4)	82
Rosa Fergani (5)	83
Musa Liam O'Brien (5)	84

Kirklevington Primary School, Kirklevington

Bibi McCoy (7)	85
Ava Irvine (7)	86
Archie Logan (7)	87
Sofia Rae Jackson (7)	88
Olive Jones (7)	89
Harriet Bowers (6)	90
Freddie Bendelow (7)	91
Imogen Heffernan (7)	92

Nina's Nursery Preschool, High Lane

Evelyn Charles (5)	93
Kenneth Hayne (7)	94

Pickhill CE Primary School, Thirsk

Erin Walsh (5)	95
Kit Dixon (4)	96
Annabelle Reade (6)	97
Imogen Burgess (6)	98
Alexander Nicholson (6)	99
Chloé Midgley (6)	100

Sandford Primary School, Sandford

Ezra Wright (6)	101
Archer Cox (6)	102
Harry Nolan (7)	103
Rafferty Bird (6)	104
Oscar Stewart (7)	105
Izzy King (7)	106
Megan Ruff (7)	107
Noah Bird (6)	108
Annie McCarthy (7)	109
Rupert Skinner (6)	110
Phoebe Britton (6)	111
Samuel Coulson (5)	112
Wilf Horton (6)	113
Hattie Bow (7)	114
Max Adams (7)	115
Arthur Jones (6)	116

Seaton Sluice First School, Seaton Sluice

Jax Madderson (7)	117
Cristian Stipa (7)	118
April Harper (6)	119
Erik Cooper (7)	120
Jacob Frier (7)	121
Artair Hutchison (7)	122
Esme Todd (6)	123
Tilly Taylor (6)	124
Isla Payne (7)	125
Georgia Gilbert (7)	126
Sophia Duffy (6)	127
Eliza Duffy (6)	128

Marina Vera Abraham (7)	129
Mason Shields (6)	130
Phoebe Burton (7)	131
Alice Nicholson (6)	132
Rowan Puttick-Newby (6)	133
Matilda Walton (7)	134
Rafael Vera Abraham (7)	135
Gracie Stokes (6)	136
Connor Carron (6)	137
Annie Marshall (6)	138

Spittal C.I.W. V.C. School, Spittal

Elijah Groves (7)	139
Isabel Griffiths (6)	140
Sienna Gardner (7)	141
Alex Perkins-Severn (6)	142
Alfie Perkins-Severn (6)	143
Ada Thomas (6)	144
Harri Chilvers (7)	145

St Francis Catholic & CE Primary School, Ventnor

Eden-Rose Hickman (7)	146
Alice Exposite (7)	147
Oliver Riley (7)	148
Mabel Brown (7)	149
Harry Sabine (6)	150
Mabel Dashwood-Wilson (6)	151

St Hilda's CE Primary School, Firswood

Elisa Merridith (6)	152
Rupert Hamill (7)	153

Westwood Academy, Hadleigh

Archie Welham (7)	154
Daisy Bartlett (7)	155
Ezra Dean (7)	156
James F (7)	157
Cooper Watts (7)	158
Eli Lewis (7)	159

Natasha Short (7)	160
Florence Kendrick (7)	161
Mason Williams (7)	162
Ollie Miller (7)	163
James Goodwin (7)	164
Benjamin Fleming (7)	165
Albie Williams (7)	166
George Connor (7)	167
Jaxon Stripe (7), Leo Legon (7) & John Cottee (6)	168
Jude Wiseman (7)	169
Wylie McQueen (6)	170

Wilson Primary School, Reading

Kingsley Yat Ming Fong (4)	171
Meriah Rajeev (4)	172
Eesa Rehman (4)	173

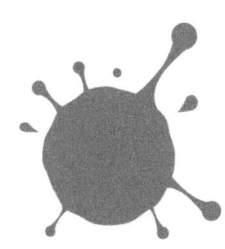

The Acrostics

Hot Chocolate

H e's a little funny, just like me,
O n his head there is whipped cream.
T all and wide, brown and white.

C olourful sprinkles on his head.
H e wears a top hat.
O n his face there are marshmallow eyes.
C ute and silly, he's always happy,
O verjoyed, and sometimes snappy.
L ong arms made of straws,
A nd legs made out of chocolate bars.
T his monster is my pet,
E veryone calls him Hot Chocolate!

Ahaan Bhavnani (6)
Alpha Preparatory School, Harrow

Bloodsucker

B lack and scary
L ives underground
O nly comes out at night
O ften eats brains
D oes naughty things
S cary and slimy
U nderground he lives
C lever and cold
K icks and is angry
E veryone is scared
R eally loud.

Vishaan Kansagra (5)
Alpha Preparatory School, Harrow

Oswald

O swald the monster
S leeps in the day
W atches TV while drinking strawberry milkshakes
A s tall as a planet
L oves ice cream with sprinkles, strawberries, raspberries, chocolate and big marshmallows on top
D oesn't like dancing!

Rohan Haria-Collins (6)
Alpha Preparatory School, Harrow

Pinkieboo

P inkie has spiky blue hair
I t loves pink and red
N eeds lots of hugs
K ind and loves to eat fruit
I s funny and cute
E ats jelly all day
B eautiful smile
O ften sleeps
O nly comes at night.

Yanle Li (5)
Alpha Preparatory School, Harrow

Tickleblue

T alks a lot
I s very smelly
C old and blue
K eeps secrets
L oves watching TV
E ats slime
B lue and soft fur
L icks me on the face
U nder the sofa
E verybody likes him.

Neil Bhudia (5)
Alpha Preparatory School, Harrow

Google

G iant claws scratching the floor.
O minous growls, a scary sound.
O ut at night it roams the sky.
G laring eyes make the night bright.
L ooking for a place where I cannot be seen.
E ww, I stepped into its slime.

Yichen Shi (7)
Alpha Preparatory School, Harrow

Cutie Boo

C lever Cutie Boo
U ses so many stickers
T ries to tickle me
I love Cutie Boo so much
E ats so much candy.

B oo! Cutie Boo
O nly loves me
O nly sleeps at night.

Jinyao Xu (6)
Alpha Preparatory School, Harrow

Purplebod

- **P** urple and playful
- **U** gly
- **R** eally scary
- **P** owerful pointy teeth
- **L** oves to eat people
- **E** vil eyes
- **B** ossy and bad!
- **O** nly comes out at night
- **D** rinks blood!

Adam Rashid (6)
Alpha Preparatory School, Harrow

Scaryboo

S leeps under my bed
C olourful and friendly
A lways happy and smiling
R ed and purple
Y ucky and kicks
B est friend
O nly loves me
O nly sleeps in the daytime.

Sai Patel (6)
Alpha Preparatory School, Harrow

Astorm

A storm is a funny monster
S port is one of his favourite subjects
T all and wild monster, he is
O h no, here comes Astorm!
R un, Astorm, run!
M onsters are not so scary.

Priyen Lakhani (7)
Alpha Preparatory School, Harrow

Evil Boss

E ats and drinks blood
V ery mean
I t lives in a cave
L oves to eat humans

B lue and bossy
O nly eats humans
S cary and mean
S leepy.

Sienna Patil (6)
Alpha Preparatory School, Harrow

Milky

M ilky is a messy monster
I ce cream is her favourite
L ollipops make her fur change colour
K angaroos love her
Y oyos are her favourite toy.

Yashvi Pindoria (7)
Alpha Preparatory School, Harrow

Batmon

B lack and scary
A nd lives in a tall castle
T eeth are sharp
M ean and moody
O nly comes out at night
N aughty and horrible!

Veer Kathrecha (6)
Alpha Preparatory School, Harrow

Flink The Funny Monster

F link the funny monster
U nder the bridge, he lives
N uts are his favourite food
N ot well-behaved
Y ellow is his favourite colour.

Daaris Siddiqui (7)
Alpha Preparatory School, Harrow

About Rusty

R usty is my monster
U nique is the way he looks
S lime is what he likes to eat
T ily is his best friend
Y ou will like my monster.

Rezaan Lasharie (7)
Alpha Preparatory School, Harrow

Furbro

F riendly and furious
U gly and terrifying
R eally mean
B ad and bold
R uns very fast
O nly comes out in the afternoon!

Khaydan Patel (6)
Alpha Preparatory School, Harrow

Joyful

J olly DJ Joyful
O nly wants happiness
Y ou never see him angry
F un vibes
U nbelievable smiles
L oves good music.

Zak Patel (6)
Alpha Preparatory School, Harrow

Pongy

P ounces on people every day
O nly comes out at night
N aughty and scary
G rabs 199 people every day
Y ellow and scary!

Dylan Kharaud-Patel (6)
Alpha Preparatory School, Harrow

Shrek

S hrek the monster.
H e likes music.
R umbles and grumbles at Donkey.
E ats slugs, worms and plants.
K ind he is.

Ryan Mara (6)
Alpha Preparatory School, Harrow

Fluffy

F riendly
L oves to eat blood
U gly and funny
F riday he comes out
F urry and fun
Y ou will like him.

Amilia Rajendram (5)
Alpha Preparatory School, Harrow

Combat

C old and clever
O range and angry
M ean and naughty
B ouncy and mean
A lways scaring
T ough and bad.

Ammar Banire (5)
Alpha Preparatory School, Harrow

Scary

S leeps in the morning
C omes out at night
A t night he eats people for dinner
R eally fast
Y ucky smell.

Purvi Udupi (5)
Alpha Preparatory School, Harrow

Loby

L ots of eyes so he can see in the dark
O ne hundred arms to feel
B lue, bumpy skin
Y ummy food to fill his tummy.

Kaiyan Patel (6)
Alpha Preparatory School, Harrow

Lunar The Monster

L oves to eat people
U nhappy with slime
N ot a friend
A n evil monster
R otten food is his favourite.

Ishaan Verma (6)
Alpha Preparatory School, Harrow

Stinky

S leeps
T ough
I nsane
N aughty
K icks
Y ucky.

Jesse Pinduria (5)
Alpha Preparatory School, Harrow

Dozy

D otty Dozy
O nly eats goo
Z aps everywhere
Y ucky and stinky.

Satvik Kashyap (5)
Alpha Preparatory School, Harrow

Untitled

K ing Monster
I s
N ot nice!
G reedy with all

M oney!
O range
N eeds
S tinky
T wo monsters
E yes are blue
R otten monster.

Eddy-Joe Kidd (7)
Callander Primary School, Bridgend

Untitled

F riendly
E ats
G reen
U nder
S limy

P urple
E yes
N ice
G rab
U ses
I s
N ice.

Noah Beaton (6)
Callander Primary School, Bridgend

Doofang

D angerous.
O nly death left!
O ften quiet.
F ingers come up from the ground!
A ngry always.
N eeds to kill.
G reedy for blood.

Louis Nicholson (7)
Callander Primary School, Bridgend

Scribbler

S cares people
C areful
R uns
I t's strong
B ig
B ouncing
L ikes to
E at meat
R eally fast.

Daniel Wood (6)
Callander Primary School, Bridgend

Ice Cream

I s it
C old?
E ats

C upcakes.
R uns fast.
E ats popcorn.
A cts good,
M ostly.

Faith Glen (6)
Callander Primary School, Bridgend

My Slimy Monster Friend

S tinky
C ute
A lways shy
R eally slimy
L oves to sleep
E ats bugs
T ries to hide all the time.

Ruby Macmillan-Rae (6)
Callander Primary School, Bridgend

Bubble

B eautiful
U gly
B ouncing
B ored
L oser
E ats poo.

M agic moon
C old.

Morven McSorley (6)
Callander Primary School, Bridgend

Stinky

S cares people
T oo kind
I t has six arms
N aughty
K eeps secrets
Y ellow hands.

Solomon Walker-Cunliffe (6)
Callander Primary School, Bridgend

Strikes The Meat-Eating Monster

S cary
T errifying
R uns
I nteresting
K ind
E ats meat
S pecial.

Fergus Picken (6)
Callander Primary School, Bridgend

Untitled

C reepy
A lways angry
V anishes
E ats people
S cary.

Joseph Cox (7)
Callander Primary School, Bridgend

Untitled

L onely but friendly
O range fur
N aughty
A nd sometimes angry.

Laura Wasyluk (7)
Callander Primary School, Bridgend

Untitled

W alks
I s
L oves
L ikes
O range
W ears.

Tilly Burke (7)
Callander Primary School, Bridgend

Clumzy Munch

C auses chaos
L ight as a kite
U lbet is a friend
M essy as a bin
Z igs and zooms everywhere
Y ells like a dinosaur

M usty as a bull
U fafa is his island
N ever stops eating
C runches on crocodiles
H is name is Clumzy Munch.

Arran Small (7)
Hazlehead Primary School, Aberdeen

Sea Beast

S caly blue body
E ats sperm whales
A ttacks other sea monsters

B ig and brave
E normous sharp claws
A nother thing it likes is attacking boats
S wims in the deepest, darkest parts of the sea
T ail is sharp and spiky.

Matthew Speagell (7)
Hazlehead Primary School, Aberdeen

Bouncing

B ouncing in Jello
O f monster wings fluttering
U nder shadows of creepiness
N ow people don't know why
C lever and smart
I n creepy caves
N aughty or nice, whatever you are
G oing home wherever you are.

Emma Axinti (7)
Hazlehead Primary School, Aberdeen

Eye Monster

E yes everywhere,
Y ellow face,
E ars are blue,

M ake people happy,
O nly eats fruit,
N ice colours,
S leeps on a bed,
T hey look cool,
E veryone knows him,
R eally beautiful.

Yaseen Hegy (7)
Hazlehead Primary School, Aberdeen

Rainbow

R eally likes rainbows and her name is Rainbow
A cts silly sometimes
I s nice and kind
N ever say Rainbow is bad to rainbows
B ouncy like jelly
O nly likes rainbows
W ears only rainbows!

Abbie Rostant (7)
Hazlehead Primary School, Aberdeen

Micee Maws

M y name is Micee Maws
I love to cuddle
C urly fur
E ating vegetables
E yes are blue

M ini horns
A lways playing
W ears blue socks
S leeps like a werewolf.

Brayden Mackie (7)
Hazlehead Primary School, Aberdeen

Sticky

S limy goo will be on you.
T welve eyes, they're creepy too,
I t's always up to mischief.
C reeping into your house.
K icks you when you're sleeping.
Y ucky goo coming out of her nose.

Anna Garrett (7)
Hazlehead Primary School, Aberdeen

My Monster

M y monster's name is Monster
O h, she is very kind
N ever trust a monster
S illy monster
T idy monster
E veryone enjoys monsters
R oar, you will see them as a surprise.

Asya Konaroglu (7)
Hazlehead Primary School, Aberdeen

Cutie Bays

C ute as a little kitten
U nicorn horn
T errifying
I hate rats
E ats wild animals

B aby cry
A dorable as a puppy
Y ucky
S cary.

Whitney Kaka (7)
Hazlehead Primary School, Aberdeen

Bobby

B ounces like a kangaroo
O range face and a dog's ears
B lue is his favourite colour
B eautiful tentacles help him swim
Y oghurt is his favourite food.

Jessica Smith (7)
Hazlehead Primary School, Aberdeen

Slimin!

S cary and slimy
L ots of feet and hands and eyes
I n a cave, a very dark cave
M akes lots of slime
I am scared of him
N ever be his friend.

Demians Blazevics (7)
Hazlehead Primary School, Aberdeen

Randirt

R ainbow as a unicorn
A bsolutely weird
N aughty as a spoiled child
D usty
I t is cloudy
R uns fast
T alks a lot.

Skye-Marie Anderson (8)
Hazlehead Primary School, Aberdeen

Shaper

S cary and slimy
H as a rainbow on it
A lways in a good mood
P lays with other monsters
E ats goo
R uns as slow as a turtle.

Jessica Cheyne (7)
Hazlehead Primary School, Aberdeen

Yellow

Y ellow spots,
E ats a lot of bugs,
L ives in a bunker,
L oves bugs,
O nly often goes out of his bunker,
W ears nothing.

Finn Teperek (7)
Hazlehead Primary School, Aberdeen

Cutey

C ute, yellow bow,
U nhappy when friends are sad,
T iny, fluffy, orange tail,
E yes are super-cute,
Y ellow sock and orange sock.

Aleksandra Firsovas (7)
Hazlehead Primary School, Aberdeen

Best Bunny

B unnies are the best
U nder stinky hay
N ibbling yummy grass
N osing around to wonder what's going on
Y ummy, yummy grass.

Rowan McKay (7)
Hazlehead Primary School, Aberdeen

Danger

D eadly monster
A ttacks people
N ever nice
G reedy and jolly
E yes with teeth around them
R eally naughty.

Jasper Houston (7)
Hazlehead Primary School, Aberdeen

Slimy

S limy and sticky
L ives in a ship
I like finding treasure
M y ship has cannons!
Y ucky, green pirate is me.

Spencer Chapman (8)
Hazlehead Primary School, Aberdeen

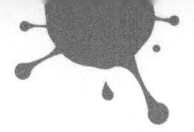

Honey

H oney is nice
O ne monster likes honey
N o one likes scary monsters
E ve is her owner
Y ay, she is happy.

Eve McCarry (7)
Hazlehead Primary School, Aberdeen

Camper

C amps a lot
A lways happy
M akes purple slime
P lays hide-and-seek
E ats poo
R uns fast.

Finn Hewitt (7)
Hazlehead Primary School, Aberdeen

Steve

S illy like a monkey
T wenty eyes
E yes are white and black
V ery stinky
E ats candy all day.

Poppy McCombie (7)
Hazlehead Primary School, Aberdeen

Bubble

B lows bubbles,
U nnoticed,
B eautiful,
B e cute,
L ikes slime,
E yes are big.

Hope Thomson (8)
Hazlehead Primary School, Aberdeen

Slimy

S illy as a monkey
L ikes to shout like a bird
I t loves to eat
M ini mouth
Y ucky teeth.

Maci Wood (8)
Hazlehead Primary School, Aberdeen

Slime

S mells bad
L ooks disgusting
I n a cave all day
M arches like a soldier
E yes are grey.

Lexi Smith (7)
Hazlehead Primary School, Aberdeen

Silly

S illy monster, Bellow
I t has one eye
L ikes cookies
L ikes apples
Y oung and fun.

Thomas Gray (7)
Hazlehead Primary School, Aberdeen

Goofy

G igantic
O ctopus arms
O ften likes to swim
F aints a lot
Y our friend.

Lewis Hume (7)
Hazlehead Primary School, Aberdeen

Bloby

B urps a lot
L oads of eyes
O range spots
B obs around
Y ellow skin.

William McAulay (7)
Hazlehead Primary School, Aberdeen

Suck

S limy
U gly as a snail
C laws like glass
K icks a lot of bums.

Manish Shatheesh (7)
Hazlehead Primary School, Aberdeen

Bacon

B ig monster
A wesome
C lumsy
O ne eye
N aughty.

Erin Macdonald (7)
Hazlehead Primary School, Aberdeen

Monster University

M y monster is called Monster, he goes to
U niversity with all his friends.

Nicholas Taylor (7)
Hazlehead Primary School, Aberdeen

Sparkly

S lime,
P ark. Lives in the park,
A pples. Loves apples,
R ed lips,
K angaroo. Her best friend is a kangaroo,
L ollipop,
Y ellow. Has yellow eyes.

Rayaan Ismail (5)
ILM Primary School, Cathays

Smiley Monster

S pecial
M elons she likes
I gloo, she visits her cousins in the igloo
L ives in the lolly shop
E lla the elephant is her cousin
Y ellow horn.

Zara Noor (5)
ILM Primary School, Cathays

Happy Monster

H appy monster I am
A ll day I like to play
P lay with my friends
P izza and apples I like
Y es I am Haroon the happy monster!

Haroon Idris (5)
ILM Primary School, Cathays

Slime Monster

S nakes; eats snakes,
L ots of legs,
I gloo; lives in an igloo,
M ountains; visits mountains,
E lephant, his best friend.

Yusuf Tahir (4)
ILM Primary School, Cathays

Slime Monster

S uper. It's super
L ion. Plays with lions
I gloo. Lives in an igloo
M elon. Eats melons
E ars. Has ears.

Faraj Islam (5)
ILM Primary School, Cathays

Raiboe, The Rainbow Monster

R ainboe
A pples
I gloo is where she lives
B est friend is Bunny
O pens doors
E lephant.

Maryam Saeed (5)
ILM Primary School, Cathays

Fluffy Monster

F ish they eat
L ollipop
U mbrella they carry
F unny faces they make
F ountain
Y o-yo.

Maryam Tarafder (4)
ILM Primary School, Cathays

Slimy Monster

S naky
L ives in a lake
I t loves to go to an igloo
M angoes it eats
Y ellow eyes it has.

Shuaib Mohamed (4)
ILM Primary School, Cathays

Happy Monster

H e has a horn. He loves to eat
A pples.
P icks pink flowers.
P owers and plays
Y oyo.

Reem Alhayfani (5)
ILM Primary School, Cathays

Sushi Monster

S ushi
U sually
S hop, love to shop
H ouse, lives in a house
I gloo.

Azees Jan De Jager Khan (4)
ILM Primary School, Cathays

Spiky Monster

S illy
P lays at the park
I gloo home
K ing
Y acht.

Muhammad Abdur Raheem (5)
ILM Primary School, Cathays

Untitled

P ink skin
I n the ground it lives
N ice
K ites it plays with.

Haneen Haseeb (4)
ILM Primary School, Cathays

Robo Monster

R ocket fast
O range leg
B each he lives on
O ranges he loves.

Bilal Aziz (4)
ILM Primary School, Cathays

Jump

J ogs in the park
U mbrella
M onkey is my best friend
P aws.

Raheem Nassar Ismail (4)
ILM Primary School, Cathays

Mimi Monster

M ummy monster,
I gloo, lives in an igloo,
M onkey,
I guana.

Rosa Fergani (5)
ILM Primary School, Cathays

Fun Monster

F ish, likes to eat fish.
U nder the sea.
N ice.

Musa Liam O'Brien (5)
ILM Primary School, Cathays

Queen Mean

Q ueen Mean of the whole world.
U sually
E ats anything.
E ats humans.
N ever nice.

M ean all the time.
E ats glasses.
A ngry all the time.
N ever weird.

Bibi McCoy (7)
Kirklevington Primary School, Kirklevington

Fireball

- **F** ierce and scary
- **I** ncredible blue wings
- **R** ed skin
- **E** normous orange bulgy eyes
- **B** ad manners
- **A** mazing loud roar
- **L** arge claws with teeth
- **L** azy and not hardworking.

Ava Irvine (7)
Kirklevington Primary School, Kirklevington

Monster Boy

M agnificent
O ily
N aughty
S ausage legs
T errifying
E ats humans
R ude

B ad guy
O wl wings
Y oghurt claws.

Archie Logan (7)
Kirklevington Primary School, Kirklevington

Monster

M onster has sharp teeth
O ne googly eye
N oodle legs
S uper smile
T remendous
E ffortlessly walks across the silky water
R ed eyes.

Sofia Rae Jackson (7)
Kirklevington Primary School, Kirklevington

Fire Eater

F lick
I nvisible
R ule breaker
E njoying

E verything
A lone
T ail
E xploding head
R osy cheeks.

Olive Jones (7)
Kirklevington Primary School, Kirklevington

Greedy

G enerous
R ainy legs
E ggy eyes
E normous teeth
D izzy daisy
Y ucky floppy horns

Harriet Bowers (6)
Kirklevington Primary School, Kirklevington

Scapy

S limy stripes.
C razy shaking.
A nxious face.
P ancake rolls.
Y ucky eyes.

Freddie Bendelow (7)
Kirklevington Primary School, Kirklevington

Yummy

Y ellow skin
U nlucky monster
M ilky Way eyes
M elted minds
Y ucky horns.

Imogen Heffernan (7)
Kirklevington Primary School, Kirklevington

Bloblob

B loblob is magical
L ong legs
O ne heart
B loblob is funny and friendly
L oves to eat plums
O n the trampoline
B ounces everywhere.

Evelyn Charles (5)
Nina's Nursery Preschool, High Lane

Spinit

S pins all day
P ractising new skills
I n-between snack breaks
N ever been afraid
I mproving all the time
T o win.

Kenneth Hayne (7)
Nina's Nursery Preschool, High Lane

Sweetness

S weetness the monster
W ears a pink and purple bracelet
E ats sweeties
E verybody's friend
T iny tail
N ever sad
E xcited
S miley
S uper kind.

Erin Walsh (5)
Pickhill CE Primary School, Thirsk

My Slimebot

S limebot the monster
L oves to scare you
I s very angry
M ud is his favourite
E ats pasta
B oo!
O ne big, scary eye
T alks in a deep voice.

Kit Dixon (4)
Pickhill CE Primary School, Thirsk

Isabel

I sabel loves huggles
S he likes to play
A nd she is really soft
B ut she is really kind
E ven when she is mad or sad
L ike when she gets hurt.

Annabelle Reade (6)
Pickhill CE Primary School, Thirsk

Floba

F urry features with a bobbly nose
L ively little monster
O ut of the darkness, he goes
B ad breath and grotty teeth
A rms swinging as he blows.

Imogen Burgess (6)
Pickhill CE Primary School, Thirsk

Loobdo Who Are You?

L oobdo is a hairy monster,
O dd,
O ld, grumpy monster,
B ig and scary monster,
D ances with his friends,
O n the stage.

Alexander Nicholson (6)
Pickhill CE Primary School, Thirsk

Chloé

C hloé is kind and caring
H appy and polite
L aughs lots
O utdoorsy
É veryone's friend.

Chloé Midgley (6)
Pickhill CE Primary School, Thirsk

Angry Scary

A ngry
N early kills
G ross
R eally wobbly teeth
Y ucky

S cary mouth
C urved teeth
A bloody cover
R ay shotgun
Y uck.

Ezra Wright (6)
Sandford Primary School, Sandford

Horrendous

H airy, horrid
O riginal
R ocket dress
R olo dress
E gg-tastic
N on-stop
D angerous
O riginal
U ndeliverable
S illy.

Archer Cox (6)
Sandford Primary School, Sandford

White

W hite eyes with no pupils,
H e doesn't sleep,
I nvisible to all,
T he monster flies,
E ating children all day and night.

Harry Nolan (7)
Sandford Primary School, Sandford

Monster

M ostly invisible
O cean lover
N ight walker
S wimmer
T ired never
E vil
R eads everything.

Rafferty Bird (6)
Sandford Primary School, Sandford

Deadly

D eadly to death
E ats people
A deadly person
D eadly hands
L oves his chainsaw
Y ellow gold.

Oscar Stewart (7)
Sandford Primary School, Sandford

Colour

C olour, the monster,
O range fluff,
L oves animals,
O range scales,
U nique,
R ed scales.

Izzy King (7)
Sandford Primary School, Sandford

Lilly

L illy the monster
I s very kind to people
L oves food
L oves drinks
Y ellow shoes on her feet.

Megan Ruff (7)
Sandford Primary School, Sandford

Lazer

L azer Cloud the monster
A scary cloud
Z ooms through the sky
E ats humans
R eally crazy.

Noah Bird (6)
Sandford Primary School, Sandford

Monster

M ean
O uch
N eedle horns
S elfish
T eeth fangs
E xtra slimy
R ude.

Annie McCarthy (7)
Sandford Primary School, Sandford

Chips

C razy hair
H e loves to eat chips
I ncredibly hungry
P olite
S plendid.

Rupert Skinner (6)
Sandford Primary School, Sandford

Gift

G reat colours
I nside is a present
F un and friendly
T ake the present it gives.

Phoebe Britton (6)
Sandford Primary School, Sandford

Laser

L aser beams
A lien eyes
S tripy top
E ight eyes
R eally terrifying!

Samuel Coulson (5)
Sandford Primary School, Sandford

Silly

S tinky
I magination
L oves tricks
L ots of colour
Y ou will laugh.

Wilf Horton (6)
Sandford Primary School, Sandford

Sticky

S limy,
T iny,
I cy,
C areful,
K ind,
Y ells loudly.

Hattie Bow (7)
Sandford Primary School, Sandford

Sian

S inging voice
I s extremely deadly
A ngry
N ightmare.

Max Adams (7)
Sandford Primary School, Sandford

Dark

D ark matter,
A ngry,
R eally angry,
K ill.

Arthur Jones (6)
Sandford Primary School, Sandford

Shin Tails From Sonic Tapes

S cary
H as orange tails,
I can fly,
N aughty,

T o find chaos emeralds,
A lways scared of Shin Sonic,
I s so big,
L ittle shoes,
S cary pink eyes.

Jax Madderson (7)
Seaton Sluice First School, Seaton Sluice

Zack From Uranus

U ses its claws to scratch.
R uns very fast to people.
A cts very scary.
N eeds to touch everything, always.
U nder a big, large, humongous rock it sleeps.
S limy, black, drippy tongue.

Cristian Stipa (7)
Seaton Sluice First School, Seaton Sluice

Bobby The Monster

Z ooms through the sky at midnight,
O range fluffy fur and the fur is super,
O n his tongue he has black spots,
M y monster is cute and kind,
S limy, stinky and yellow teeth.

April Harper (6)
Seaton Sluice First School, Seaton Sluice

Pizzaroni Monster

H as a spiky chain arm
I s super fast
D oes the shuffle dance
E ats pizza
O ften scares people
U gly, indigo skin
S o scary, run away!

Erik Cooper (7)
Seaton Sluice First School, Seaton Sluice

Ghosty The Monster

S leeps in the day
M ean and scary
E ats a lot of disgusting bugs
L ooks really scary
L ots of slime comes off his hands
Y ells a lot.

Jacob Frier (7)
Seaton Sluice First School, Seaton Sluice

Gizmo

G rowling in the pitch black
I t lives in a swamp
Z ig-zag claws on its hands and feet
M akes people have nightmares
O nly eats gooey slime.

Artair Hutchison (7)
Seaton Sluice First School, Seaton Sluice

Yellow Monster

Y ellow body
E ats rainbow candy and lollipops
L ittle pink bow
L ikes to swim underwater
O ften naughty
W alks very fast.

Esme Todd (6)
Seaton Sluice First School, Seaton Sluice

Mia The Flower Monster

F riendly monster
L oves to swim
O range wings
W ill always help others
E veryone loves her
R eally big eye.

Tilly Taylor (6)
Seaton Sluice First School, Seaton Sluice

Burgy

B ig, greasy hands
U ses a fork and spoon to pick up objects
R anch sauce
G ooey, green lettuce
Y es, unusually cheesy.

Isla Payne (7)
Seaton Sluice First School, Seaton Sluice

Bobby, Willow's Friend

B ig, blue, three eyes
O range legs
B eautiful spots on its body
B lobs of slime
Y ucky gloop hanging from its mouth.

Georgia Gilbert (7)
Seaton Sluice First School, Seaton Sluice

Snowy Bobby

S melly breath! Yuck!
N ice clothes
O range spots all over
W hen he moves you can smell him
Y ellow nails and teeth.

Sophia Duffy (6)
Seaton Sluice First School, Seaton Sluice

Slimy

S limy, green forehead
L ikes goo
I t has dark blue fur
M any different smells
Y ellow, sharp, razor fangs.

Eliza Duffy (6)
Seaton Sluice First School, Seaton Sluice

Fangs

F riendly monster
A nd has fangs
N eeds to eat slime
G reen and blue horns
S ays *roar!*

Marina Vera Abraham (7)
Seaton Sluice First School, Seaton Sluice

Cave Monster

C olourful spikes on his back,
A lways very hungry
V ery dark, green claws,
E ats green and blue things.

Mason Shields (6)
Seaton Sluice First School, Seaton Sluice

Friend

F urry
R ainbow colour
I s funny
E ats noodles
N aughty
D oes love to fly.

Phoebe Burton (7)
Seaton Sluice First School, Seaton Sluice

Kindness Monster

K ind monster
I t is a spotty monster
N ever scares anyone
D rinks very gooey slime.

Alice Nicholson (6)
Seaton Sluice First School, Seaton Sluice

Bobby The Monster

B eautiful
O ften naughty
B ouncing in the air
B lue eyes
Y ucky smell.

Rowan Puttick-Newby (6)
Seaton Sluice First School, Seaton Sluice

Cleo The Monster

C heerful and clever
L ikes slimy blobs
E ats gloomy dots
O ften jumpy and hyper.

Matilda Walton (7)
Seaton Sluice First School, Seaton Sluice

Rory The Monster

R eally rude
O nly eats meat
R un away
Y ucky, he's so smelly!

Rafael Vera Abraham (7)
Seaton Sluice First School, Seaton Sluice

Mean

M y monster is cheeky
E ats slimy jelly
A ngry monster
N aughty.

Gracie Stokes (6)
Seaton Sluice First School, Seaton Sluice

Cave Monster

C laws are sharp
A lways angry
V ery scary
E vil orange eyes.

Connor Carron (6)
Seaton Sluice First School, Seaton Sluice

Bob The Monster

B right orange fur
O nly eats olives
B lack eyes.

Annie Marshall (6)
Seaton Sluice First School, Seaton Sluice

Monsters

M any live in my bedroom
O h what a fright I received
N o one took any notice, surely I should be believed
S o I took them on a journey
T aking my whole class and my teacher
E ven grown-ups could see this imaginary creature
R oar!
S eeing is believing. Now run before he eats ya!

Elijah Groves (7)
Spittal C.I.W. V.C. School, Spittal

Monsters

M onsters have orange around their tummy
O ld gold monsters with sharp claws
k **N** obbly knees and toes
S cary eyes
T eeth as yellow as a banana
E lectrified monster that goes *zap* and *ping*
R ed tummy as big and round as an apple
S tumpy monster goes home now.

Isabel Griffiths (6)
Spittal C.I.W. V.C. School, Spittal

Monster

M agic, dancing monsters
O pen their giant eyes
N oisy, nature music beat
S tomping, hairy, rainbow feet
T wisting and twirling every day
E nding only with the rising sun
R esting quietly after all that fun!

Sienna Gardner (7)
Spittal C.I.W. V.C. School, Spittal

Monsters

M agnificent king monster
O rders his guards ot fight
N o one is safe
S top the attack on our day
T errifying attack
E very monster needs to be present
R un to safety
S uper monster wins the day.

Alex Perkins-Severn (6)
Spittal C.I.W. V.C. School, Spittal

Monsters

M onsters are screaming,
O range scary monster,
N ever touch a monster,
S am hates monsters,
T ogether we scare them,
E very monster,
R ed colourful monster,
S peedy monsters.

Alfie Perkins-Severn (6)
Spittal C.I.W. V.C. School, Spittal

Monsters

M oon-shaped face,
O range and grey legs,
N oisy, funny roar,
S mall sparkling eyes,
T angled, knotty fur,
E lephant-heavy feet,
R ainbow teeth smile,
S queezy and cuddly.

Ada Thomas (6)
Spittal C.I.W. V.C. School, Spittal

Monsters

M y monster is mysterious
O range and red
N ever naughty but...
S ometimes scary
T errific teeth
E xtraordinary energy and a
R eally funny guy.

Harri Chilvers (7)
Spittal C.I.W. V.C. School, Spittal

Eggracula

E ggracula the monster.
G ood friend to all.
G ot sharp teeth.
R olls in the snow.
A nd bumped his head.
C an fly like a bat.
U gly crack on his head.
L oves to play.
A nd the best in the world.

Eden-Rose Hickman (7)
St Francis Catholic & CE Primary School, Ventnor

My Silly Monster

P laying is what he likes to do
E ating space slime
I n his space world
Z ooming around Planet Earth
E arth seems silly to him
N ever-ending pranks for Peizen.

Alice Exposite (7)
St Francis Catholic & CE Primary School, Ventnor

Sluck

S luck is a terrifying monster
L oves eating bones
U sually found in a dark cave
C an scare kids in their beds
K ids will scream when Sluck gets near them.

Oliver Riley (7)
St Francis Catholic & CE Primary School, Ventnor

Monster Acrostics - Poetic Creatures

Happy

H appy is hilarious,
A nd very stinky too!
P erfect hugs he gives,
P ecking is his favourite thing.
Y ou will get a great little gift from him.

Mabel Brown (7)
St Francis Catholic & CE Primary School, Ventnor

Binny

B inny loves rubbish
I t eats all the time
N othing goes to waste
N ever full up
Y esterday, Binny ate the bin.

Harry Sabine (6)
St Francis Catholic & CE Primary School, Ventnor

Love

L oves to bake,
O ne eye,
V ersus a friendly monster,
E veryone loves a monster!

Mabel Dashwood-Wilson (6)
St Francis Catholic & CE Primary School, Ventnor

Terrible

T errible
E ats everything
R ounder and rounder and
R ounder his belly grows
I don't know if he will stay
B igger and bigger he grows
L ooking down on everyone until
E ventually, he pops and goes to Heaven.

Elisa Merridith (6)
St Hilda's CE Primary School, Firswood

Monster Acrostics - Poetic Creatures

Danger

W arden likes getting wet,
A lways treat Warden with loyalty,
R ed and blue are Warden's favourite colours,
D eep in a swamp is where Warden lives,
E very Warden has three eyes,
N ever wake Warden up or else...

Rupert Hamill (7)
St Hilda's CE Primary School, Firswood

The Terrible Black Monster Poem

M onsters are terrible and the teeth
O h no! Monsters are crawling over Bob
N o, they're terrible and scary
S uper scary, teeth as sharp as knives
T wo-faced, half-zombie and half-vampire
E vil laser eyes and swollen
R evolution into the terrible monster.

Archie Welham (7)
Westwood Academy, Hadleigh

The Black Terrifying Monster

M onsters were in my dream last night.
O kay, they lost me before they got me!
N ow I'm fine, phew. They nearly ate me!
S cary! Scary! Help, they found me!
T eeth as rough as a knife, what do I do?
E verywhere, what can I do?
R eally, really scary!

Daisy Bartlett (7)
Westwood Academy, Hadleigh

Evil

M onsters are evil, have ten eyes
O h, no! So horrifying, it's blue
N early ate everybody
S o scary it has blood eyes
T eeth as sharp as knives
E ating blood, it is half zombie
R evolting, scary monsters.

Ezra Dean (7)
Westwood Academy, Hadleigh

The Monster Apocalypse

M y head has been devoured.
O kay, they can't see me... No!
N ever came Frankenstein.
S o came Dracula.
T he bloodthirsty vampires came!
E very single zombie's flesh was rotten.
R ed bloody tarantula.

James F (7)
Westwood Academy, Hadleigh

The Terrifying Club

M onsters are terrifying.
O h no, monsters are after us!
N o! They're going to suck our blood.
S uper-frightening.
T eeth as sharp as knives.
E vil monsters.
R evolting monsters.

Cooper Watts (7)
Westwood Academy, Hadleigh

Super Scary Monsters

M onsters are scary
O h no! They're coming to eat us
N o!
S uper scary monsters are coming!
T eeth as sharp as knives
E very type of monster is scary
R un, they're coming!

Eli Lewis (7)
Westwood Academy, Hadleigh

Evil, Scary Monsters

M onsters are frightening
O h, what is that?
N early got me!
S top and hide from the thing!
T eeth are so sharp.
E vil, scary eyes.
R un away from the monster!

Natasha Short (7)
Westwood Academy, Hadleigh

Monster Of Terror

M onsters are scary...
O h no!
N early got me
S tinky breath and spikes!
T error comes when I see a monster
E very monster is creepy
R *ooooar!*

Florence Kendrick (7)
Westwood Academy, Hadleigh

Monsters

M onsters are scary.
O h no, they are under my bed.
N early ate me.
S uper scary.
T eeth as sharp as knives.
E vil as criminals.
R evolting monster.

Mason Williams (7)
Westwood Academy, Hadleigh

The Big Monsters

M onsters are terrifying
O h my gosh!
N ow there is a head zombie
S tinky monsters
T he big zombie is snoring in the house
E vil monsters
R otten.

Ollie Miller (7)
Westwood Academy, Hadleigh

Run Away Or You Die!

M onsters are beasts!
O h no, they ate my favourite toy!
N ooooo!
S uper creepy!
T errible babies too!
E at your brains!
R evolting monsters!

James Goodwin (7)
Westwood Academy, Hadleigh

Monsterville

M onsters have terrifying tentacles
O h no!
N early got me
S cary monsters
T errible monsters
E vil red eyes
R evolting monsters!

Benjamin Fleming (7)
Westwood Academy, Hadleigh

Monster Chaos, Please Stop!

M onsters are scary
O h my gosh!
N o, please don't eat me!
S top!
T errifying monsters
E rax monsters
R oar! Growl!

Albie Williams (7)
Westwood Academy, Hadleigh

Oh No, Monsters

M onsters are ridiculously silly
O h no, they're throwing icicles
N oooooooo!
S cary!
T errifying
E xtra scary!
R evolting!

George Connor (7)
Westwood Academy, Hadleigh

Monsters

M onsters are scary,
O h no!
N early ate me,
S uper scary!
T eeth as sharp as knives,
E vil, swollen eyes,
R evolting monsters.

Jaxon Stripe (7), Leo Legon (7) & John Cottee (6)
Westwood Academy, Hadleigh

Untitled

M onsters are haunted,
O h, help!
N o, some have blood,
S word teeth,
T errifying ghosts,
E vil zombie,
R un away!

Jude Wiseman (7)
Westwood Academy, Hadleigh

Monster Poem

M onster
O h, uh
N o!
S top
T errifying
E vil monsters
R evolting.

Wylie McQueen (6)
Westwood Academy, Hadleigh

Funny

F unny monster
U sually loves to eat popcorn
N o ears
N o nose
Y ellow skin.

Kingsley Yat Ming Fong (4)
Wilson Primary School, Reading

Tock

T errifying
O rdinary
C rawly
K ing.

Meriah Rajeev (4)
Wilson Primary School, Reading

Daz

D raws on people
A lways silly
Z ooms.

Eesa Rehman (4)
Wilson Primary School, Reading

Young Writers Information

We hope you have enjoyed reading this book – and that you will continue to in the coming years.

If you're the parent or family member of an enthusiastic poet or story writer, do visit our website **www.youngwriters.co.uk/subscribe** and sign up to receive news, competitions, writing challenges and tips, activities and much, much more! There's lots to keep budding writers motivated!

If you would like to order further copies of this book, or any of our other titles, then please give us a call or order via your online account.

Young Writers
Remus House
Coltsfoot Drive
Peterborough
PE2 9BF
(01733) 890066
info@youngwriters.co.uk

Join in the conversation!
Tips, news, giveaways and much more!

YoungWritersUK   YoungWritersCW
youngwriterscw   youngwriterscw

Scan Me!